DREAMY COCOONS

Wrap that precious baby in the very essence of love! Your affection will combine with every stitch you crochet to make these warm sets. A soft cocoon, paired with a matching cap, beret, or hat, will keep a newborn to three-month-old infant cozy and comfy. The six designs range from truly simple to slightly more intricate, so no matter your skill level with a crochet hook, you're sure to find the perfect pattern!

About Kim Kotary

Kim Kotary is a freelance designer and Craft Yarn Council of America Certified Instructor who lives in New York. In her profession, Kim touches almost every imaginable aspect of fabric and fibers. Her master's degree in textile conservation has led to exciting long-term projects, such as working with a large private collection of kimonos. Kim also designs and writes patterns for a yarn company and has published several books on crochet. As an instructor, she travels locally to teach a wide range of fiber arts. For more about Kim's work, visit www.kkotary.webs.com.

LEISURE ARTS, INC.
Little Rock, Arkansas

Purple Textures

Finished Size
Cocoon: 22" long x 30" circumference (56 x 76 cm)
Cap: Fits Newborn to 3 months

MATERIALS
Medium Weight Yarn (MEDIUM 4)
[3 ounces, 145 yards
(85 grams, 133 meters) per skein]:
    Variegated - 3 skeins
[3.5 ounces, 170 yards
(100 grams, 156 meters) per skein]:
    Purple - 1 skein
Crochet hook, size K (6.5 mm) **or** size needed
    for gauge
Yarn needle

GAUGE: In pattern, 12 sc and 11 rnds = 4" (10 cm)

Gauge Swatch: 3" (7.5 cm) wide x 7¹/₂" (19 cm) long
Work same as Cocoon through Rnd 4.

STITCH GUIDE
DECREASE
    Pull up a loop in each of next 2 sc, YO and draw
    through all 3 loops on hook **(counts as one sc)**.

COCOON

Rnd 1 (Right side): With Variegated, ch 2, insert hook in second ch from hook, YO and pull up a loop, YO and draw through one loop on hook (ch made), YO and draw through both loops on hook (first sc made), ★ insert hook in ch at base of previous sc, YO and pull up a loop, YO and draw through one loop on hook (ch made), YO and draw through both loops on hook (sc made); repeat from ★ 14 times **more**, place marker in last sc made for st placement, sc in each ch across opposite side; do **not** join, place marker to mark beginning of rnd *(see Markers, page 33)*: 32 sc.

Rnd 2: 2 Sc in **both** loops of next sc, [sc in Front Loop Only of next sc *(Fig. 3, page 34)*, sc in Back Loop Only of next sc] across to marked sc, 2 sc in **both** loops of each of next 2 sc, move marker to second sc of 4-sc group just made, (sc in Front Loop Only of next sc, sc in Back Loop Only of next sc) across to last sc, 2 sc in **both** loops of last sc: 36 sc.

Rnd 3: 2 Sc in **both** loops of next sc, (sc in Back Loop Only of next sc, sc in Front Loop Only of next sc) across to marked sc, 2 sc in **both** loops of each of next 2 sc, move marker to second sc of 4-sc group just made, (sc in Back Loop Only of next sc, sc in Front Loop Only of next sc) across to last sc, 2 sc in **both** loops of last sc: 40 sc.

Rnds 4-13: Repeat Rnds 2 and 3, 5 times; removing second marker as Rnd 13 is worked: 80 sc.

Rnd 14: (Decrease, ch 2) around: 40 sc and 40 ch-2 sps.

Rnds 15-20: Pull up a loop in next sc and in next ch-2 sp, YO and draw through all 3 loops on hook **(counts as one sc)**, ch 2, ★ pull up a loop in same ch-2 sp as last sc made and in next ch-2 sp, YO and draw through all 3 loops on hook **(counts as one sc)**, ch 2; repeat from ★ around.

Rnd 21: Sc in each sc and in each ch-2 sp around: 80 sc.

Instructions continued on page 4.

Rnd 22: (Sc in Front Loop Only of next sc, sc in Back Loop Only of next sc) around.

Rnd 23: (Sc in Back Loop Only of next sc, sc in Front Loop Only of next sc) around.

Rnds 24-28: Repeat Rnds 22 and 23 twice, then repeat Rnd 22 once **more**.

Rnds 29-51: Repeat Rnds 14-28 once, then repeat Rnds 14-21 once **more**; at end of Rnd 51, slip st in next sc, finish off.

BAND

Rnd 1: With **wrong** side facing, join Purple with sc in same st as last slip st *(see Joining With Sc, page 33)*; sc in each sc around; do **not** join, place marker to mark beginning of rnd: 80 sc.

Rnd 2: Sc in Back Loop Only of each sc around.

Rnds 3-6: (Sc in Front Loop Only of next sc, sc in Back Loop Only of next sc) around.

Rnd 7: Ch 1, slip st in both loops of each sc around; join with slip st to first slip st, finish off.

CAP

Rnd 1 (Right side)**:** With Purple and leaving a long end for sewing, ch 2, 3 sc in second ch from hook; do **not** join, place marker to mark beginning of rnd.

Note: Mark Rnd 1 as **right** side.

Rnd 2: 2 Sc in each sc around: 6 sc.

Rnd 3: (2 Sc in next sc, sc in next sc) around: 9 sc.

Rnd 4: (2 Sc in next sc, sc in next 2 sc) around: 12 sc.

Rnd 5: (2 Sc in next sc, sc in next 3 sc) around: 15 sc.

Rnd 6: (2 Sc in next sc, sc in next 4 sc) around: 18 sc.

Rnd 7: (2 Sc in next sc, sc in next 5 sc) around: 21 sc.

Rnd 8: ★ 2 Sc in **both** loops of next sc, (sc in Front Loop Only of next sc, sc in Back Loop Only of next sc) 3 times; repeat from ★ 2 times **more**: 24 sc.

Rnd 9: ★ 2 Sc in **both** loops of next sc, sc in Front Loop Only of next sc, (sc in Back Loop Only of next sc, sc in Front Loop Only of next sc) 3 times; repeat from ★ 2 times **more**: 27 sc.

Rnd 10: ★ 2 Sc in **both** loops of next sc, (sc in Front Loop Only of next sc, sc in Back Loop Only of next sc) 4 times; repeat from ★ 2 times **more**: 30 sc.

Rnds 18-22: Pull up a loop in next sc and in next ch-2 sp, YO and draw through all 3 loops on hook **(counts as one sc)**, ch 2, ★ pull up a loop in same ch-2 sp as last sc made and in next ch-2 sp, YO and draw through all 3 loops on hook **(counts as one sc)**, ch 2; repeat from ★ around.

Rnd 23: Sc in each sc and in each ch-2 sp around: 36 sc.

Rnds 24-26: (Sc in Back Loop Only of next sc, sc in Front Loop Only of next sc) around; at end of Rnd 26, slip st in next sc, finish off.

BRIM

Rnd 1: With **wrong** side facing and working in Back Loops Only, join Variegated with sc in same st as last slip st; sc in each sc around; do **not** join, place marker to mark beginning of rnd: 36 sc.

Rnds 2 and 3: (Sc in Front Loop Only of next sc, sc in Back Loop Only of next sc) around; at end of Rnd 3, slip st in next sc, finish off.

Thread yarn needle with long end at top. Using photo as as guide, sew tip of Cap down.

Fold up Brim.

Rnd 11: ★ 2 Sc in **both** loops of next sc, sc in Front Loop Only of next sc, (sc in Back Loop Only of next sc, sc in Front Loop Only of next sc) 4 times; repeat from ★ 2 times **more**: 33 sc.

Rnd 12: ★ 2 Sc in **both** loops of next sc, (sc in Front Loop Only of next sc, sc in Back Loop Only of next sc) 5 times; repeat from ★ 2 times **more**: 36 sc.

Rnds 13-16: (Sc in Back Loop Only of next sc, sc in Front Loop Only of next sc) around.

Rnd 17: (Decrease, ch 2) around: 18 sc and 18 ch-2 sps.

Orange Flower

Finished Size
Cocoon: 24" long x 28½" circumference
(61 x 72.5 cm)
Bonnet: Fits Newborn to 3 months

MEDIUM 4

MATERIALS
Medium Weight Yarn
[6 ounces, 315 yards
(170 grams, 288 meters) per skein]:
  Peach - 2 skeins
  Orange - 1 skein
Crochet hook, size H (5 mm) **or** size needed
  for gauge

GAUGE: 3 repeats (18 sts) = 4¾" (12 cm);
         8 rnds/rows = 3¾" (9.5 cm)

Gauge Swatch: 5½" (14 cm) diameter
Work same as Cocoon through Rnd 5.

STITCH GUIDE

BACK POST SINGLE CROCHET *(abbreviated BPsc)*
Insert hook from **back** to **front** around post of dc
indicated *(Fig. 5, page 34)*, YO and pull up a loop,
YO and draw through both loops on hook. Skip
stitch in front of BPsc.
FOUNDATION SINGLE CROCHET *(abbreviated Fsc)*
★ Insert hook in ch at base of last sc made, YO and
pull up a loop, YO and draw through one loop on
hook **(ch made)**, YO and draw through both loops
on hook **(sc made)**; repeat from ★ for each Fsc.
DECREASE
Pull up a loop in each of next 2 sts, YO and draw
through all 3 loops on hook.

COCOON

Rnd 1 (Right side): With Peach, ch 4, 11 dc in fourth
ch from hook; join with slip st to top of beginning
ch-4: 12 sts.

Note: Loop a short piece of yarn around any stitch to
mark Rnd 1 as **right** side.

Rnd 2: Ch 3 **(counts as first dc, now and throughout)**,
dc in same st, 2 dc in next dc and in each dc around;
join with slip st to first dc: 24 dc.

Rnd 3: Ch 1, sc in same st, skip next dc, 5 dc in next
dc, skip next dc, ★ sc in next dc, skip next dc, 5 dc in
next dc, skip next dc; repeat from ★ around; join with
slip st to first sc: 36 sts.

Rnd 4: Ch 3, 2 dc in same st, skip next 2 dc, sc in next
dc, skip next 2 dc, ★ 5 dc in next sc, skip next 2 dc, sc
in next dc, skip next 2 dc; repeat from ★ around, 2 dc
in same st as first dc; join with slip st to first dc.

Rnd 5: Ch 3, 2 dc in same st, skip next dc, sc in next
dc, 5 dc in next sc, sc in next dc, skip next dc, ★ 5 dc
in next dc, skip next dc, sc in next dc, 5 dc in next sc,
sc in next dc, skip next dc; repeat from ★ around,
2 dc in same st as first dc; join with slip st to first dc,
finish off: 72 sts.

Instructions continued on page 8.

Rnd 6: With **right** side facing, join Orange with sc in same st as joining *(see Joining With Sc, page 33)*; skip next 2 dc, 5 dc in next sc, skip next 2 dc, ★ sc in next dc, skip next 2 dc, 5 dc in next sc, skip next 2 dc; repeat from ★ around; join with slip st to first sc, finish off.

Rnd 7: With **right** side facing and working in Back Loops Only *(Fig. 3, page 34)*, join Peach with slip st in same st as joining; ch 3, 2 dc in same st, sc in next dc, skip next dc, 5 dc in next dc, skip next dc, sc in next dc, 5 dc in next sc, skip next 2 dc, sc in next dc, skip next 2 dc, ★ 5 dc in next sc, sc in next dc, skip next dc, 5 dc in next dc, skip next dc, sc in next dc, 5 dc in next sc, skip next 2 dc, sc in next dc, skip next 2 dc; repeat from ★ around, 2 dc in same st as first dc; join with slip st to first dc: 108 sts.

Rnd 8: Ch 1, working in both loops, sc in same st, skip next 2 dc, 5 dc in next sc, skip next 2 dc, ★ sc in next dc, skip next 2 dc, 5 dc in next sc, skip next 2 dc; repeat from ★ around; join with slip st to first sc.

Rnd 9: Ch 3, 2 dc in same st, skip next 2 dc, sc in next dc, skip next 2 dc, ★ 5 dc in next sc, skip next 2 dc, sc in next dc, skip next 2 dc; repeat from ★ around, 2 dc in same st as first dc; join with slip st to first dc, finish off.

Rnd 10: With **right** side facing, skip first 3 sts and join Orange with slip st in next sc; ch 3, 3 dc in same st, skip next 2 dc, work BPsc around next dc, skip next 2 dc, ★ 7 dc in next sc, skip next 2 dc, work BPsc around next dc, skip next 2 dc; repeat from ★ around; 3 dc in same st as joining; join with slip st to first dc, finish off: 144 sts.

Rnd 11: With **right** side facing, join Peach with slip st in first BPsc; ch 3, 2 dc in same st, skip next 3 dc, work BPsc around next dc, skip next 3 dc, ★ 5 dc in next BPsc, skip next 3 dc, work BPsc around next dc, skip next 3 dc; repeat from ★ around, 2 dc in same st as joining; join with slip st to first dc: 108 sts.

Rnd 12: Ch 1, sc in same st, skip next 2 dc, 5 dc in next st, skip next 2 dc, ★ sc in next dc, skip next 2 dc, 5 dc in next st, skip next 2 dc; repeat from ★ around; join with slip st to first sc.

Rnd 13: Ch 3, 2 dc in same st, skip next 2 dc, sc in next dc, skip next 2 dc, ★ 5 dc in next sc, skip next 2 dc, sc in next dc, skip next 2 dc; repeat from ★ around, 2 dc in same st as first dc; join with slip st to first dc.

Rnds 14 and 15: Repeat Rnds 12 and 13; at end of Rnd 15, finish off.

Rnd 16: Repeat Rnd 10: 144 sts.

Rnd 17: With **right** side facing, join Peach with slip st in first BPsc; ch 3, 2 dc in same st, skip next 3 dc, work BPsc around next dc, skip next 3 dc, ★ 5 dc in next BPsc, skip next 3 dc, work BPsc around next dc, skip next 3 dc; repeat from ★ around, 2 dc in same st as joining; join with slip st to first dc: 108 sts.

Rnd 18: Ch 1, sc in same st, skip next 2 dc, 5 dc in next st, skip next 2 dc, ★ sc in next dc, skip next 2 dc, 5 dc in next st, skip next 2 dc; repeat from ★ around; join with slip st to first sc.

Rnd 19: Ch 3, 2 dc in same st, skip next 2 dc, sc in next dc, skip next 2 dc, ★ 5 dc in next sc, skip next 2 dc, sc in next dc, skip next 2 dc; repeat from ★ around, 2 dc in same st as first dc; join with slip st to first dc.

Rnds 20-23: Repeat Rnds 18 and 19 twice; at end of Rnd 23, finish off.

Rnd 24: Repeat Rnd 10: 144 sts.

Rnd 25: With **right** side facing, join Peach with slip st in first BPsc; ch 3, 2 dc in same st, skip next 3 dc, work BPsc around next dc, skip next 3 dc, ★ 5 dc in next BPsc, skip next 3 dc, work BPsc around next dc, skip next 3 dc; repeat from ★ around, 2 dc in same st as joining; join with slip st to first dc: 108 sts.

Rnd 26: Ch 1, sc in same st, skip next 2 dc, 5 dc in next st, skip next 2 dc, ★ sc in next dc, skip next 2 dc, 5 dc in next st, skip next 2 dc; repeat from ★ around; join with slip st to first sc.

Rnd 27: Ch 3, 2 dc in same st, skip next 2 dc, sc in next dc, skip next 2 dc, ★ 5 dc in next sc, skip next 2 dc, sc in next dc, skip next 2 dc; repeat from ★ around, 2 dc in same st as first dc; join with slip st to first dc.

Rnds 28-33: Repeat Rnds 26 and 27, 3 times; at end of Rnd 33, finish off.

Rnd 34: Repeat Rnd 10: 144 sts.

Rnd 35: With **right** side facing, join Peach with slip st in first BPsc; ch 3, 2 dc in same st, skip next 3 dc, work BPsc around next dc, skip next 3 dc, ★ 5 dc in next BPsc, skip next 3 dc, work BPsc around next dc, skip next 3 dc; repeat from ★ around, 2 dc in same st as joining; join with slip st to first dc: 108 sts.

Rnd 36: Ch 1, sc in same st, skip next 2 dc, 5 dc in next st, skip next 2 dc, ★ sc in next dc, skip next 2 dc, 5 dc in next st, skip next 2 dc; repeat from ★ around; join with slip st to first sc.

Rnd 37: Ch 3, 2 dc in same st, skip next 2 dc, sc in next dc, skip next 2 dc, ★ 5 dc in next sc, skip next 2 dc, sc in next dc, skip next 2 dc; repeat from ★ around, 2 dc in same st as first dc; join with slip st to first dc.

Rnds 38-45: Repeat Rnds 36 and 37, 4 times; at end of Rnd 45, finish off.

Rnd 46: Repeat Rnd 10: 144 sts.

Rnd 47: With **right** side facing, join Peach with slip st in first BPsc; ch 3, 2 dc in same st, skip next 3 dc, work BPsc around next dc, skip next 3 dc, ★ 5 dc in next BPsc, skip next 3 dc, work BPsc around next dc, skip next 3 dc; repeat from ★ around, 2 dc in same st as joining; join with slip st to first dc: 108 sts.

Rnd 48: Ch 1, sc in same st, skip next 2 dc, 3 dc in next BPsc, skip next 2 dc, ★ sc in next dc, skip next 2 dc, 3 dc in next BPsc, skip next 2 dc; repeat from ★ around; join with slip st to first sc, do **not** finish off: 72 sts.

RUFFLE

Rnd 1: Ch 3, **turn**; working in Back Loops Only, dc in same st, sc in next st, (3 dc in next st, sc in next st) around, dc in same st as first dc; join with slip st to first dc, finish off: 144 sts.

Rnd 2: With **wrong** side facing and working in both loops, join Orange with sc in any sc; skip next dc, 5 dc in next dc, skip next dc, ★ sc in next sc, skip next dc, 5 dc in next dc, skip next dc; repeat from ★ around; join with slip st to first sc, finish off.

EDGING

Rnd 1: With **right** side facing and working in free loops of sts on Rnd 48 behind Ruffle *(Fig. 2a, page 34)*, join Orange with sc in any st; sc in next st and in each st around; join with slip st to first sc.

Rnd 2: Ch 1, sc in same st and in each sc around; join with slip st to first sc.

Rnd 3: Ch 1; working from **left** to **right**, work reverse sc in each sc around *(Figs. 7a-d, page 35)*; join with slip st to first st, finish off.

Instructions continued on page 10.

BONNET
CROWN

Work same as Cocoon, page 6, through Rnd 5: 72 sts.

Rnd 6: With **right** side facing, join Orange with sc in same st as joining; skip next 2 dc, 7 dc in next sc, skip next 2 dc, ★ work BPsc around next dc, skip next 2 dc, 7 dc in next sc, skip next 2 dc; repeat from ★ around; join with slip st to first sc, finish off: 96 sts.

SIDE

Row 1: With **right** side facing, join Peach with slip st in same st as joining; ch 3, 2 dc in same st, skip next 3 dc, work BPsc around next dc, ★ skip next 3 dc, 5 dc in next BPsc, skip next 3 dc, work BPsc around next dc; repeat from ★ 8 times **more**, skip next 3 dc, 3 dc in next BPsc, leave remaining 15 sts unworked: 61 sts.

Row 2: Ch 1, turn; sc in first dc, ★ ch 2, skip next 2 dc, dc in next BPsc, ch 2, skip next 2 dc, sc in next dc; repeat from ★ across: 21 sts and 20 ch-2 sps.

Row 3: Ch 3, turn; 2 dc in first sc, skip next ch-2 sp, sc in next dc, ★ skip next ch-2 sp, 5 dc in next sc, skip next ch-2 sp, sc in next dc; repeat from ★ across to last ch-2 sp, skip last ch-2 sp, 3 dc in last sc: 61 sts.

Rows 4-8: Repeat Rows 2 and 3 twice, then repeat Row 2 once **more**: 21 sts and 20 ch-2 sps.

Row 9: Ch 3, turn; 2 dc in first sc, ★ skip next ch-2 sp, sc in next dc, skip next ch-2 sp, 3 dc in next sc; repeat from ★ across, do **not** finish off: 43 sts.

RUFFLE

Row 1: Ch 3, turn; working in Back Loops Only, 2 dc in first dc, (sc in next st, 3 dc in next dc) across; finish off: 87 sts.

Place a marker around first dc on Row 1 for st placement.

Row 2: With **right** side facing, join Orange with slip st in marked dc, do **not** remove marker; ch 3, 2 dc in same st, skip next 2 dc, sc in next sc, ★ skip next dc, 5 dc in next dc, skip next dc, sc in next sc; repeat from ★ across to last 3 dc, skip next 2 dc, (2 dc, ch 3, slip st) in last dc; finish off.

First Tie: With Orange, ch 2, sc in second ch from hook, work 49 Fsc; working in chs across opposite side, 2 sc in first ch, sc in each ch across; do **not** finish off.

Neck Trim: With **right** side facing, folding Ruffle against **right** side of Side, and working through both thicknesses, slip st in end of first row (through Row 1 of Ruffle and Row 9 of Side); ch 1, working in end of remaining rows on Side, (sc in next row, skip next row, 5 dc in next row, skip next row) twice; working in sts across Rnd 6 of Crown, sc in same BPsc as dc on Row 1 of Side, skip next 3 dc, 5 dc in next dc, skip next 3 dc, sc in next BPsc, skip next 3 dc, 5 dc in next dc, skip next 3 dc, sc in same sc as dc on Row 1 of Side; working in end of rows on Side, skip first row, 5 dc in next row, skip next row, sc in next row, skip next row, 5 dc in next row, skip next row, sc in next row; folding against **right** side of Side, slip st in end of last row working through both thicknesses, do **not** finish off.

Second Tie: Insert hook in same row as last slip st on Neck Trim, YO and pull up a loop, YO and draw through one loop on hook **(ch made)**, YO and draw through both loops on hook **(sc made)**, work 49 Fsc; working in chs across opposite side, 2 sc in first ch, sc in each ch across; do **not** finish off.

Trim: Working in free loops of Row 9 of Side, sc in first st, (decrease, sc in next st) across; join with slip st to first sc on First Tie; ch 1, working from **left** to **right**, work reverse sc in each st across to Second Tie; finish off.

Tan Plaid

 **INTERMEDIATE**

Finished Size
Cocoon: 24" long x 31" circumference (61 x 78.5 cm)
Hat: Fits Newborn to 3 months

MATERIALS
Medium Weight Yarn **MEDIUM 4**
[3.5 ounces, 200 yards
(100 grams, 182 meters) per skein]:
   Tan - 3 skeins
   Brown - 3 skeins
Crochet hook, size H (5 mm) **or** size needed
   for gauge
Yarn needle

GAUGE: In pattern, 14 sts and 15 rows = 4" (10 cm)

Gauge Swatch: 4" (10 cm) diameter
Work same as Cocoon through Rnd 8.

STITCH GUIDE
FRONT POST DOUBLE CROCHET *(abbreviated FPdc)*
YO, insert hook from **front** to **back** around post of
FPtr indicated, YO and pull up a loop, (YO and draw
through 2 loops on hook) twice *(Fig. 5, page 34)*.
FRONT POST TREBLE CROCHET *(abbreviated FPtr)*
YO twice, insert hook from **front** to **back** around
post of st indicated, YO and pull up a loop, (YO and
draw through 2 loops on hook) 3 times *(Fig. 5,
page 34)*. Do **not** skip sc behind FPtr unless
indicated.
DECREASE
Pull up a loop in each of next 2 sc, YO and draw
through both loops on hook **(counts as one sc)**.

COCOON

Rnd 1 (Right side): With Tan, ch 2, 6 sc in second ch
from hook; join with slip st to first sc.

Note: Loop a short piece of yarn around any stitch to
mark Rnd 1 as **right** side.

Rnd 2: Ch 1, 2 sc in Back Loop Only of each sc around
(Fig. 3, page 34); join with slip st to first ch, drop Tan
to **wrong** side: 12 sc.

Carry unused yarn on **wrong** side of piece.

Rnd 3: With Brown, ch 1, sc in Back Loop Only of first
sc, working in **front** of previous rnd *(Fig. 6, page 35)*,
dc in free loop of first sc on Rnd 1 *(Fig. 2a, page 34)*,
★ sc in Back Loop Only of next 2 sc, working in **front**
of previous rnd, dc in free loop of next sc on Rnd 1;
repeat from ★ around to last sc, sc in Back Loop Only
of last sc; join with slip st to first ch: 12 sc and 6 dc.

Instructions continued on page 14.

Rnd 4: Ch 1, working in Back Loops Only, sc in first sc, 2 sc in next dc, (sc in next 2 sc, 2 sc in next dc) around to last sc, sc in last sc; join with slip st to first ch, drop Brown: 24 sc.

Rnd 5: With Tan, ch 1, sc in Back Loop Only of first 4 sc, working in **front** of previous rnd, dc in free loop of next sc on Rnd 2, ★ sc in Back Loop Only of next 4 sc, working in **front** of previous rnd, dc in free loop of next sc on Rnd 2 repeat from ★ around; join with slip st to first ch: 24 sc and 6 dc.

Continue to work sc in Back Loops Only of sts on previous rnd.

Rnd 6: Ch 1, sc in first 4 sc, 2 sc in next dc, (sc in next 4 sc, 2 sc in next dc) around; join with slip st to first ch, drop Tan: 36 sc.

Rnd 7: With Brown, ch 1, sc in first 2 sc, work FPtr around next dc 4 rnds **below**, (sc in next 6 sc, work FPtr around next dc 4 rnds **below**) around to last 4 sc, sc in last 4 sc; join with slip st to first ch: 36 sc and 6 FPtr.

Rnd 8: Ch 1, sc in first 2 sc, 2 sc in next FPtr, (sc in next 6 sc, 2 sc in next FPtr) around to last 4 sc, sc in last 4 sc; join with slip st to first ch, drop Brown: 48 sc.

Rnd 9: With Tan, ch 1, sc in first 7 sc, work FPtr around next dc 4 rnds **below**, (sc in next 8 sc, work FPtr around next dc 4 rnds **below**) around to last sc, sc in last sc; join with slip st to first ch: 48 sc and 6 FPtr.

Rnd 10: Ch 1, sc in first 7 sc, 2 sc in next FPtr, (sc in next 8 sc, 2 sc in next FPtr) around to last sc, sc in last sc; join with slip st to first ch, drop Tan: 60 sc.

Work FPtr around FPtr 4 rnds **below** throughout, unless otherwise indicated.

Rnd 11: With Brown, ch 1, sc in first 3 sc, work FPtr around next FPtr, (sc in next 10 sc, work FPtr around next FPtr) around to last 7 sc, sc in last 7 sc; join with slip st to first ch: 60 sc and 6 FPtr.

Rnd 12: Ch 1, sc in first 3 sc, 2 sc in next FPtr, (sc in next 10 sc, 2 sc in next FPtr) around to last 7 sc, sc in last 7 sc; join with slip st to first ch, drop Brown: 72 sc.

Rnd 13: With Tan, ch 1, sc in first 10 sc, work FPtr around next FPtr, (sc in next 12 sc, work FPtr around next FPtr) around to last 2 sc, sc in last 2 sc; join with slip st to first ch: 72 sc and 6 FPtr.

Rnd 14: Ch 1, sc in first 10 sc, 2 sc in next FPtr, (sc in next 12 sc, 2 sc in next FPtr) around to last 2 sc, sc in last 2 sc; join with slip st to first ch, drop Tan: 84 sc.

Rnd 15: With Brown, ch 1, sc in first 4 sc, work FPtr around next FPtr, (sc in next 14 sc, work FPtr around next FPtr) around to last 10 sc, sc in last 10 sc; join with slip st to first ch: 84 sc and 6 FPtr.

Rnd 16: Ch 1, sc in first 4 sc, 2 sc in next FPtr, (sc in next 14 sc, 2 sc in next FPtr) around to last 10 sc, sc in last 10 sc; join with slip st to first ch, drop Brown: 96 sc.

Rnd 17: With Tan, ch 1, sc in first 13 sc, work FPtr around next FPtr, (sc in next 16 sc, work FPtr around next FPtr) around to last 3 sc, sc in last 3 sc; join with slip st to first ch: 96 sc and 6 FPtr.

Rnd 18: Ch 1, sc in first 13 sc, 2 sc in next FPtr, (sc in next 16 sc, 2 sc in next FPtr) around to last 3 sc, sc in last 3 sc; join with slip st to first ch, drop Tan: 108 sc.

Rnd 19: With Brown, ch 1, sc in first 5 sc, work FPtr around next FPtr, skip sc behind FPtr just made, ★ sc in next 17 sc, work FPtr around next FPtr, skip sc behind FPtr just made; repeat from ★ around to last 12 sc, sc in last 12 sc; join with slip st to first ch: 102 sc and 6 FPtr.

Rnd 20: Ch 1, sc in each st around; join with slip st to first ch, drop Brown: 108 sc.

Rnd 21: With Tan, ch 1, sc in first 14 sc, work FPtr around next FPtr, skip sc behind FPtr just made, ★ sc in next 17 sc, work FPtr around next FPtr, skip sc behind FPtr just made; repeat from ★ around to last 3 sc, sc in last 3 sc; join with slip st to first ch: 102 sc and 6 FPtr.

Rnd 22: Ch 1, sc in each st around; join with slip st to first ch, drop Tan: 108 sc.

Repeat Rnds 19-22 until piece measures approximately 22" (56 cm) from beginning, **or** to 2" (5 cm) less than desired length, ending by working Rnd 21.

Next Rnd: Ch 1, sc in first 14 sc, work FPdc around next FPtr, ★ sc in next 17 sc, work FPdc around next FPtr; repeat from ★ around to last 3 sc, sc in last 3 sc; join with slip st to first ch, cut Tan.

Last Rnd: With Brown, ch 1, sc in first 5 sc, work FPtr around next FPtr, skip sc behind FPtr just made, ★ sc in next 17 sts, work FPtr around next FPtr, skip sc behind FPtr just made; repeat from ★ around to last 12 sc, sc in last 12 sc; join with slip st to first ch, finish off leaving a long end for sewing.

CUFF

Row 1 (Right side): With Tan, ch 2, [insert hook in second ch from hook, YO and pull up a loop, YO and draw through one loop on hook **(ch made)**, YO and draw through both loops on hook **(sc made)]**, ★ insert hook in ch at base of last sc made, YO and pull up a loop **(ch made)**, YO and draw through one loop on hook, YO and draw through both loops on hook **(sc made)**; repeat from ★ 23 times **more**: 25 sc.

Row 2: Ch 1, turn; working in Back Loops Only, sc in first sc, ★ insert hook in same st as previous st, YO and pull up a loop, insert hook in next st, YO and draw through st and both loops on hook; repeat from ★ across to last sc, sc in last sc, drop Tan.

Rows 3 and 4: With Brown, repeat Row 2 twice; at end of Row 4, drop Brown.

Rows 5 and 6: With Tan, repeat Row 2 twice.

Repeat Rows 3-6 until Cuff measures same as top edge of Cocoon, ending by working Row 4.

Cut Tan and finish off Brown, leaving a long end for sewing; whipstitch ends together **(Fig. 9, page 35)**. Thread yarn needle with long end on Cocoon and sew end of rows of Cuff to last rnd of Cocoon. Fold Cuff down.

Instructions continued on page 16.

CAP
SIDE (Make 2)
Work same as Cocoon, page 12, through Rnd 10: 60 sc.

Begin working in rows.

Row 1 (Right side)**:** With Brown, ch 1, working in Back Loops Only, sc in first 3 sc, work FPtr around next FPtr, (sc in next 10 sc, work FPtr around next FPtr) 3 times, sc in next 3 sc, leave last 24 sc unworked: 36 sc and 4 FPtr.

Row 2: Ch 1, turn; sc in Front Loop Only of each st across, drop Brown: 40 sc.

Row 3: With Tan, ch 1, turn; working Back Loops Only, sc in first 9 sc, work FPtr around next FPtr, skip sc behind FPtr just made, ★ sc in next 10 sc, work FPtr around next FPtr, skip sc behind FPtr just made; repeat from ★ once **more**, sc in last 8 sc: 37 sc and 3 FPtr.

Row 4: Ch 1, turn; sc in Front Loop Only of each st across, drop Tan: 40 sc.

Row 5: With Brown, ch 1, turn; working in Back Loops Only, sc in first 3 sc, work FPtr around next FPtr, skip sc behind FPtr just made, ★ sc in next 10 sc, work FPtr around next FPtr, skip sc behind FPtr just made; repeat from ★ 2 times **more**, sc in last 3 sc: 36 sc and 4 FPtr.

Row 6: Ch 1, turn; sc in Front Loop Only of each st across; cut Brown: 40 sc.

Row 7: Repeat Row 3; finish off leaving a long end for sewing.

With **wrong** sides together, whipstitch Row 7 of both pieces together, matching sts and working through inside loops only.

EDGING & TIES
With **wrong** side facing, join Brown with slip st in end of first row of Side; ch 1, work 11 sc evenly spaced across end of rows, **turn**; working in Back Loops Only, decrease, (sc in next sc, decrease) 3 times, † working in unworked sts on Rnd 10, sc in next 7 sc, work FPtr around next FPtr, skip sc behind FPtr just made, sc in next 4 sc, [insert hook in next sc, YO and pull up a loop, YO and draw through one loop on hook **(ch made)**, YO and draw through both loops on hook **(sc made)**], ★ insert hook in ch at base of last sc made, YO and pull up a loop, YO and draw through one loop on hook **(ch made)**, YO and draw through both loops on hook **(sc made)**; repeat from ★ 28 times **more**; working in chs across opposite side, 2 sc in first ch, sc in each ch across; working in unworked sts on Rnd 10, sc in next 4 sc, work FPtr around next FPtr, skip sc behind FPtr just made, sc in next 6 sc †; work 15 sc evenly spaced across end of rows; repeat from † to † once; join with slip st to next sc, finish off.

Yellow Puffs

 **EASY**

Finished Size
Cocoon: 24" long x 26" circumference (61 x 66 cm)
Beret: Fits Newborn to 3 months

MATERIALS
Medium Weight Yarn **MEDIUM 4**
[6 ounces, 315 yards
(170 grams, 288 meters) per skein]:
  Yellow - 3 skeins
  Gold - 1 skein
Crochet hook, size H (5 mm) **or** size needed
  for gauge

GAUGE SWATCH: 4" (10 cm) diameter
Work same as Body through Rnd 3.

STITCH GUIDE
BEGINNING PUFF STITCH
(abbreviated Beginning Puff St)
Slip st in sp indicated, ch 2, ★ YO, insert hook in same sp, YO and pull up a loop; repeat from ★ once **more**, YO and draw through all 5 loops on hook.

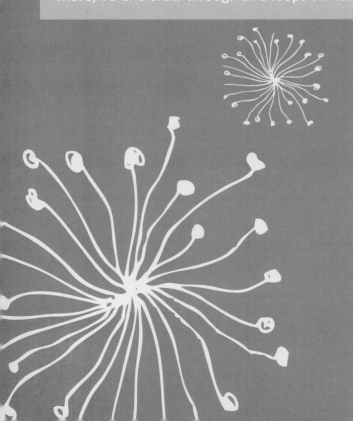

PUFF STITCH *(abbreviated Puff St)*
★ YO, insert hook in st or sp indicated, YO and pull up a loop; repeat from ★ 2 times **more**, YO and draw through all 7 loops on hook.
DECREASE (uses 2 ch-1 sps)
★ YO, insert hook in **next** ch-1 sp, YO and pull up a loop, YO, insert hook in **same** sp, YO and pull up a loop; repeat from ★ once **more**, YO and draw through all 9 loops on hook **(counts as one Puff St)**.

COCOON
Rnd 1 (Right side): With Yellow, ch 4, 11 dc in fourth ch from hook **(3 skipped chs count as first dc)**; join with slip st to first dc: 12 dc.

Note: Loop a short piece of yarn around any stitch to mark Rnd 1 as **right** side.

Rnd 2: Work Beginning Puff St in sp **before** next dc *(Fig. 4, page 34)*, ch 1, dc in next dc, ★ work Puff St in sp **before** next dc, ch 1, dc in next dc; repeat from ★ around; join with slip st to top of Beginning Puff St: 24 sts and 12 ch-1 sps.

Rnd 3: Work Beginning Puff St in next ch-1 sp, ch 1, work Puff St in next dc, ch 1, skip next Puff St, ★ work Puff St in next ch-1 sp, ch 1, work Puff St in next dc, ch 1, skip next Puff St; repeat from ★ around; join with slip st to top of Beginning Puff St: 24 Puff Sts and 24 ch-1 sps.

Rnd 4: Work Beginning Puff St in next ch-1 sp, ch 1, skip next Puff St, ★ work Puff St in next ch-1 sp, ch 1, skip next Puff St; repeat from ★ around; join with slip st to top of Beginning Puff St.

Rnd 5: Work (Beginning Puff St, ch 1, Puff St) in next ch-1 sp, ch 1, skip next Puff St, (work Puff St in next ch-1 sp, ch 1, skip next Puff St) twice, ★ (work Puff St, ch 1) twice in next ch-1 sp, skip next Puff St, (work Puff St in next ch-1 sp, ch 1, skip next Puff St) twice; repeat from ★ around; join with slip st to top of Beginning Puff St: 32 Puff Sts and 32 ch-1 sps.

Instructions continued on page 20.

Rnd 6: Work (Beginning Puff St, ch 1, Puff St) in next ch-1 sp, ch 1, skip next Puff St, (work Puff St in next ch-1 sp, ch 1, skip next Puff St) 3 times, ★ (work Puff St, ch 1) twice in next ch-1 sp, skip next Puff St, (work Puff St in next ch-1 sp, ch 1, skip next Puff St) 3 times; repeat from ★ around; join with slip st to top of Beginning Puff St: 40 Puff Sts and 40 ch-1 sps.

Rnd 7: Work (Beginning Puff St, ch 1, Puff St) in next ch-1 sp, ch 1, skip next Puff St, (work Puff St in next ch-1 sp, ch 1, skip next Puff St) 4 times, ★ (work Puff St, ch 1) twice in next ch-1 sp, skip next Puff St, (work Puff St in next ch-1 sp, ch 1, skip next Puff St) 4 times; repeat from ★ around; join with slip st to top of Beginning Puff St: 48 Puff Sts and 48 ch-1 sps.

Rnd 8: Work (Beginning Puff St, ch 1, Puff St) in next ch-1 sp, ch 1, skip next Puff St, (work Puff St in next ch-1 sp, ch 1, skip next Puff St) 5 times, ★ (work Puff St, ch 1) twice in next ch-1 sp, skip next Puff St, (work Puff St in next ch-1 sp, ch 1, skip next Puff St) 5 times; repeat from ★ around; join with slip st to top of Beginning Puff St: 56 Puff Sts and 56 ch-1 sps.

Rnd 9: Work (Beginning Puff St, ch 1, Puff St) in next ch-1 sp, ch 1, skip next Puff St, (work Puff St in next ch-1 sp, ch 1, skip next Puff St) 6 times, ★ (work Puff St, ch 1) twice in next ch-1 sp, skip next Puff St, (work Puff St in next ch-1 sp, ch 1, skip next Puff St) 6 times; repeat from ★ around; join with slip st to top of Beginning Puff St: 64 Puff Sts and 64 ch-1 sps.

Rnds 10-19: Work Beginning Puff St in next ch-1 sp, ch 1, skip next Puff St, ★ work Puff St in next ch-1 sp, ch 1, skip next Puff St; repeat from ★ around; join with slip st to top of Beginning Puff St.

Rnd 20: Work Beginning Puff St in next ch-1 sp, ch 1, (skip next Puff St, work Puff St in next ch-1 sp, ch 1) 5 times, decrease, ch 1, skip next Puff St, ★ (work Puff St in next ch-1 sp, ch 1, skip next Puff St) 6 times, decrease, ch 1, skip next Puff St; repeat from ★ around; join with slip st to top of Beginning Puff St: 56 Puff Sts and 56 ch-1 sps.

Rnds 21-25: Work Beginning Puff St in next ch-1 sp, ch 1, skip next Puff St, ★ work Puff St in next ch-1 sp, ch 1, skip next Puff St; repeat from ★ around; join with slip st to top of Beginning Puff St.

Rnd 26: Work Beginning Puff St in next ch-1 sp, ch 1, (skip next Puff St, work Puff St in next ch-1 sp, ch 1) 4 times, decrease, ch 1, skip next Puff St, ★ (work Puff St in next ch-1 sp, ch 1, skip next Puff St) 5 times, decrease, ch 1, skip next Puff St; repeat from ★ around; join with slip st to top of Beginning Puff St: 48 Puff Sts and 48 ch-1 sps.

Rnds 27-52: Work Beginning Puff St in next ch-1 sp, ch 1, skip next Puff St, ★ work Puff St in next ch-1 sp, ch 1, skip next Puff St; repeat from ★ around; join with slip st to top of Beginning Puff St; at end of Rnd 52, finish off.

BAND

Rnd 1: With **right** side facing, join Gold with slip st in any ch-1 sp; ch 3 **(counts as first hdc plus ch 1, now and throughout)**, (hdc in next ch-1 sp, ch 1) around; join with slip st to first hdc: 48 hdc and 48 ch-1 sps.

Rnds 2-8: Slip st in first ch-1 sp, ch 3, (hdc in next ch-1 sp, ch 1) around; join with slip st to first hdc.

Rnd 9: Ch 1, sc in same st and in each hdc and each ch-1 sp around; join with slip st to first sc: 96 sc.

Rnd 10: Ch 1; working from **left** to **right**, work reverse sc in each sc around *(Figs. 7a-d, page 35)*; join with slip st to first st, finish off.

BERET

Rnd 1 (Right side)**:** With Yellow, ch 3, 7 hdc in third ch from hook **(2 skipped chs count as first hdc)**; join with slip st to first hdc: 8 hdc.

Note: Mark Rnd 1 as **right** side.

Rnd 2: Work (Beginning Puff St, ch 1, Puff St) in sp **before** next hdc, ch 1, ★ (work Puff St, ch 1) twice in sp **before** next hdc; repeat from ★ around; join with slip st to top of Beginning Puff St: 16 Puff Sts and 16 ch-1 sps.

HAT

Rnds 1-7: Work same as Cocoon, page 22, through Rnd 7: 60 sc.

Rnd 8: Ch 1, 2 sc in same st, sc in next 4 sc, decrease, sc in next 3 sc, ★ 3 sc in next sc, sc in next 4 sc, decrease, sc in next 3 sc; repeat from ★ around, sc in same st as first sc; join with slip st to **both** loops of first sc: 66 sc.

Rnd 9: Ch 1, 2 sc in **both** loops of same st, sc in next 4 sc, skip next 2 sc, sc in next 4 sc, ★ (2 sc, ch 2, 2 sc) in **both** loops of next sc, sc in next 4 sc, skip next 2 sc, sc in next 4 sc; repeat from ★ around, 2 sc in **both** loops of same st as first sc, hdc in first sc to form last ch-2 sp: 72 sc and 6 ch-2 sps.

Rnd 10: Ch 1, sc in last ch-2 sp made and in next 5 sc, skip next 2 sc, sc in next 5 sc, ★ (sc, ch 2, sc) in next ch-2 sp, sc in next 5 sc, skip next 2 sc, sc in next 5 sc; repeat from ★ around, sc in same sp as first sc, hdc in first sc to form last ch-2 sp.

Repeat Rnd 10 for pattern until Hat measures approximately 7" (18 cm) from beginning **or** to desired length.

Finish off.

RUFFLE

Rnd 1: With **right** side facing, join Green with sc in any ch-2 sp *(see Joining With Sc, page 33)*; ch 3, (sc, ch 3) 4 times in same sp, (sc, ch 3) 3 times in next sc and in each sc around, working (sc, ch 3) 5 times in each ch-2 sp; join with slip st to first sc, finish off.

Blue Tunisian

Finished Size
Cocoon: 25" long x 26" circumference (63.5 x 66 cm)
Cap: Fits Newborn to 3 months

MATERIALS
Medium Weight Yarn
[4 ounces, 204 yards
(113 grams, 187 meters) per skein]:
    Variegated - 3 skeins
[5 ounces, 256 yards
(142 grams, 234 meters) per skein]:
    Blue - 1 skein
Double ended Tunisian hook, size K (6.5 mm) **or** size
    needed for gauge
Standard crochet hook, size K (6.5 mm)
Split-ring marker
Yarn needle

We recommend working the gauge swatch to learn the technique of working Tunisian Stitch in the round with a double ended crochet hook. We used Blue for the first ball of yarn and Tan for the second ball of yarn for our sample.

GAUGE: In pattern, 14 sts and 14 rnds = 4" (10 cm)

Gauge Swatch: 4" long x 8¹/₂" circumference
                    (10 x 21.5 cm)

With Blue and using double ended hook, ch 30; being careful **not** to twist ch, join with slip st to form a ring, place marker in loop on hook to mark beginning of rnd and **right** side *(Fig. A)*. Marked loop counts as first vertical bar.

Fig. A

Rnd 1
Step A: Working in back ridge of beginning ch *(Fig. 1, page 34)*, (insert hook in next ch, YO and pull up a loop) 14 times, leave remaining 15 chs unworked *(Fig. B)*: 15 loops on hook.

Fig. B

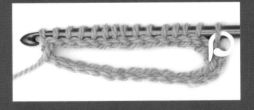

Instructions continued on page 28.

Step B: Drop Blue, turn work around; slide loops to opposite end of hook *(Fig. C)*; with Tan, **[**YO and draw through 2 loops on hook *(Figs. D & E)***]** across until 2 loops remain on hook.

Fig. C

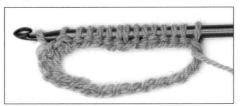

Fig. D   **Fig. E**

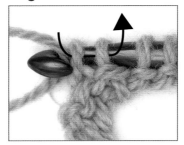   

Step C: Drop Tan, turn work around; slide last 2 loops to opposite end of hook; with Blue and working in back ridge of beginning ch, (insert hook in next ch, YO and pull up a loop) 15 times: 17 loops on hook.
Step D: Drop Blue, turn work around; slide loops to opposite end of hook; with Tan, (YO and draw through 2 loops on hook) across until 2 loops remain on hook.

Rnd 2

Step A: Drop Tan, turn work around; slide last 2 loops to opposite end of hook, insert hook under marked vertical bar *(Fig. F)*; with Blue, YO and pull up a loop, move marker to loop just made *(Fig. G)*, (insert hook under next vertical bar, YO and pull up a loop) 14 times: 17 loops on hook.

Fig. F   **Fig. G**

Step B: Drop Blue, turn work around; slide loops to opposite end of hook; with Tan, (YO and draw through 2 loops on hook) across until 2 loops remain on hook.
Step C: Drop Tan, turn work around; slide last 2 loops to opposite end of hook; with Blue, (insert hook under next vertical bar, YO and pull up a loop) 15 times: 17 loops on hook.
Step D: Drop Blue, turn work around; slide loops to opposite end of hook; with Tan, (YO and draw through 2 loops on hook) across until 2 loops remain on hook: 30 vertical bars.

Rnds 3-14: Repeat Rnd 2, 12 times; at end of Rnd 14, with Tan, YO and draw through last 2 loops; finish off, cut Blue.

STITCH GUIDE
BACK POST DOUBLE CROCHET
 (abbreviated BPdc)
YO, insert hook from **back** to **front** around post of st indicated *(Fig. 5, page 34)*, YO and pull up a loop (3 loops on hook), (YO and draw through 2 loops on hook) twice. Skip st in front of BPdc.
FRONT POST DOUBLE CROCHET
 (abbreviated FPdc)
YO, insert hook from **front** to **back** around post of st indicated *(Fig. 5, page 34)*, YO and pull up a loop (3 loops on hook), (YO and draw through 2 loops on hook) twice. Skip st behind FPdc.
BODY DECREASE
Insert hook under each of next 2 bars, YO and pull up a loop *(Fig. H)* **(counts as one st)**.

Fig. H

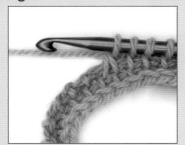

SINGLE CROCHET DECREASE
(abbreviated sc decrease)
Pull up a loop in each of next 2 sts, YO and draw through all 3 loops on hook **(counts as one sc)**.

DOUBLE CROCHET DECREASE
(abbreviated dc decrease) (uses next 2 sts)
★ YO, insert hook in **next** st, YO and pull up a loop, YO and draw through 2 loops on hook; repeat from ★ once **more**, YO and draw through all 3 loops on hook **(counts as one dc)**.

FRONT POST DECREASE *(abbreviated FP decrease)*
★ YO, insert hook from **front** to **back** around post of **next** dc *(Fig. 5, page 34)*, YO and pull up a loop, YO and draw through 2 loops on hook; repeat from ★ once **more**, YO and draw through all 3 loops on hook **(counts as one FPdc)**.

BACK POST DECREASE *(abbreviated BP decrease)*
★ YO, insert hook from **back** to **front** around post of **next** dc *(Fig. 5, page 34)*, YO and pull up a loop, YO and draw through 2 loops on hook; repeat from ★ once **more**, YO and draw through all 3 loops on hook **(counts as one BPdc)**.

COCOON
BODY

Use two separate skeins of Variegated yarn throughout Body which will be noted in the instructions as first yarn and second yarn.

With first yarn and using double ended hook, ch 94; being careful **not** to twist ch, join with slip st to form a ring, place marker in loop on hook to mark beginning of rnd and **right** side. Marked loop counts as first vertical bar.

Rnd 1
Step A: Working in back ridge of beginning ch *(Fig. 1, page 34)*, (insert hook in next ch, YO and pull up a loop) 46 times, leave remaining 47 chs unworked: 47 loops on hook.
Step B: Drop first yarn, turn work around; slide loops to opposite end of hook; with second yarn, (YO and draw through 2 loops on hook) across until 2 loops remain on hook.
Step C: Drop second yarn, turn work around; slide last 2 loops to opposite end of hook; with first yarn and working in back ridge of beginning ch, (insert hook in next ch, YO and pull up a loop) 47 times: 49 loops on hook.

Step D: Drop first yarn, turn work around; slide loops to opposite end of hook; with second yarn, (YO and draw through 2 loops on hook) across until 2 loops remain on hook.

Rnd 2
Step A: Drop second yarn, turn work around; slide last 2 loops to opposite end of hook; insert hook under marked vertical bar, with first yarn, YO and pull up a loop, move marker to loop just made, (insert hook under next vertical bar, YO and pull up a loop) 46 times: 49 loops on hook.
Step B: Drop first yarn, turn work around; slide loops to opposite end of hook; with second yarn, (YO and draw through 2 loops on hook) across until 2 loops remain on hook.
Step C: Drop second yarn, turn work around; slide last 2 loops to opposite end of hook, with first yarn, (insert hook under next vertical bar, YO and pull up a loop) 47 times: 49 loops on hook.
Step D: Drop first yarn, turn work around; slide loops to opposite end of hook; with second yarn, (YO and draw through 2 loops on hook) across until 2 loops remain on hook: 94 vertical bars.

Repeat Rnd 2 for pattern until Body measures approximately 22" (56 cm) from beginning ring.

BOTTOM
Rnd 1 (Decrease rnd)
Step A: Drop second yarn, turn work around; slide last 2 loops to opposite end of hook, with first yarn, insert hook under marked vertical bar **and** under next vertical bar, YO and pull up a loop **(first Body decrease made)**, move marker to loop just made, (insert hook under next vertical bar, YO and pull up a loop) 23 times, work Body decrease, (insert hook under next vertical bar, YO and pull up a loop) 20 times: 47 loops on hook.

Step B: Repeat Step B of Body Rnd 2.

Instructions continued on page 30.

Step C: Drop second yarn, turn work around; slide last 2 loops to opposite end of hook; with first yarn, (insert hook under next vertical bar, YO and pull up a loop) 3 times, ★ work Body decrease, (insert hook under next vertical bar, YO and pull up a loop) 20 times; repeat from ★ once **more**: 47 loops on hook.
Step D: Drop first yarn, turn work around; slide loops to opposite end of hook; with second yarn, (YO and draw through 2 loops on hook) across until 2 loops remain on hook: 90 vertical bars.

Rnd 2 (Decrease rnd)
Step A: Drop second yarn, turn work around; slide last 2 loops to opposite end of hook; with first yarn, insert hook under marked vertical bar **and** under next vertical bar, YO and pull up a loop **(first Body decrease made)**, move marker to loop just made, ★ (insert hook under next vertical bar, YO and pull up a loop) 13 times, work Body decrease; repeat from ★ 2 times more: 45 loops on hook.
Step B: Repeat Step B of Body Rnd 2.
Step C: Drop second yarn, turn work around; slide last 2 loops to opposite end of hook; with first yarn, (insert hook under next vertical bar, YO and pull up a loop) 13 times, ★ work Body decrease, (insert hook under next vertical bar, YO and pull up a loop) 13 times; repeat from ★ once **more**: 43 loops on hook.
Step D: Drop first yarn, turn work around; slide loops to opposite end of hook; with second yarn, (YO and draw through 2 loops on hook) across until 2 loops remain on hook: 84 vertical bars.

Rnds 3-12: Decrease in same manner (working 6 Body decreases per rnd), pulling up one less loop between decreases: 24 vertical bars.

Rnd 13: Work Body decrease around; cut second yarn: 12 vertical bars.

Rnd 14: (Pull up a loop under **each** of next 2 vertical bars, YO and draw through all 3 loops on hook) 6 times; finish off leaving a long end for sewing.

Thread yarn needle with long end and sew opening closed.

BAND

Rnd 1: With **right** side facing, working in free loops of beginning ch *(Fig. 2b, page 34)*, and using standard hook, join Blue with slip st in first ch; ch 3 **(counts as first dc, now and throughout)**, dc in next 3 chs, (dc decrease, dc in next 3 chs) around; join with slip st to first dc: 76 dc.

Rnd 2: [Slip st from **back** to **front** around first dc, ch 3 **(beginning BPdc made)**], work FPdc around next dc, ★ work BPdc around next dc, work FPdc around next dc, work BP decrease, work FPdc around next dc, work BPdc around next dc, work FP decrease; repeat from ★ around to last 2 dc, work BPdc around next dc, work FPdc around last dc; join with slip st to first BPdc: 58 sts.

Rnds 3-10: Work beginning BPdc around beginning BPdc, work FPdc around next FPdc, (work BPdc around next BPdc, work FPdc around next FPdc) around; join with slip st to first dc; at end of Rnd 10, finish off.

Fold Band down.

HAT
BODY

Use one skein **each** of Variegated and Blue throughout Body of Hat.

With Variegated and using double ended hook, ch 55; being careful **not** to twist ch, join with slip st to form ring, place marker in loop on hook to mark beginning of rnd and **right** side. Marked loop counts as first vertical bar.

Rnd 1
Step A: Working in back ridge of beginning ch, (insert hook in next ch, YO and pull up a loop) 27 times, leave remaining 27 chs unworked: 28 loops on hook.
Step B: Drop Variegated, turn work around; slide loops to opposite end of hook; with Blue, (YO and draw through 2 loops on hook) across until 2 loops remain on hook.
Step C: Drop Blue, turn work around; slide last 2 loops to opposite end of hook, with Variegated and working in back ridge of beginning ch, (insert hook in next ch, YO and pull up a loop) 27 times: 29 loops on hook.

Rnd 7 (Decrease rnd)
Step A: Drop Blue, turn work around; slide last 2 loops to opposite end of hook; with Variegated, insert hook under marked vertical bar **and** under next vertical bar, YO and pull up a loop **(Body decrease made)**, move marker to loop just made, ★ (insert hook under next vertical bar, YO and pull up a loop) 9 times, work Body decrease; repeat from ★ once **more**: 23 loops on hook.
Step B: Repeat Step B of Body Rnd 2.
Step C: Drop Blue, turn work around; slide last 2 loops to opposite end of hook; with Variegated, (insert hook under next vertical bar, YO and pull up a loop) 9 times, ★ work Body decrease, (insert hook under next vertical bar, YO and pull up a loop) 9 times; repeat from ★ once **more**: 31 loops on hook.
Step D: Drop Variegated, turn work around; slide loops to opposite end of hook; with Blue, (YO and draw through 2 loops on hook) across until 2 loops remain on hook: 50 vertical bars.

Rnds 8-12: Decrease in same manner (working 6 Body decreases per rnd), pulling up one less loop between decreases: 20 vertical bars.

Rnd 13: Work Body decrease around; cut Blue: 10 vertical bars.

Rnd 14: (Pull up a loop under **each** of next 2 vertical bars, YO and draw through all 3 loops on hook) 5 times; finish off leaving a long end for sewing.

Thread yarn needle with long end and sew opening closed.

BAND

Rnd 1: With **right** side facing, working in free loops of beginning ch, and using standard hook, join Blue with sc in first ch; sc in next ch and in each ch around; do **not** join, place marker to mark beginning of rnd *(see Markers, page 33)*: 55 sc.

Rnd 2: (Sc in next 9 sc, sc decrease) around: 50 sc.

Rnd 3: Sc in each sc around.

Instructions continued on page 32.

Step D: Drop Variegated, turn work around; slide loops to opposite end of hook; with Blue, (YO and draw through 2 loops on hook) across until 2 loops remain on hook: 55 vertical bars.

Rnds 2-6
Step A: Drop Blue, turn work around; slide last 2 loops to opposite end of hook, insert hook under marked vertical bar; with Variegated, YO and pull up a loop, move marker to loop just made (insert hook under next vertical bar, YO and pull up a loop) 26 times: 29 loops on hook.
Step B: Drop Variegated, turn work around; slide loops to opposite end of hook; with Blue, (YO and draw through 2 loops on hook) across until 2 loops remain on hook.
Step C: Drop Blue, turn work around; slide last 2 loops to opposite end of hook; with Variegated, (insert hook under next vertical bar, YO and pull up a loop) 28 times: 30 loops on hook.
Step D: Drop Variegated, turn work around; slide loops to opposite end of hook, with Blue, (YO and draw through 2 loops on hook) across until 2 loops remain on hook: 55 vertical bars.

BRIM

Row 1 (Right side): Ch 1, **turn**; working in Back Loops Only *(Fig. 3, page 34)*, sc in next 16 sc, leave remaining 34 sc unworked.

Rows 2-7: Ch 1, turn; skip first sc, working in both loops, sc in next sc and in each sc across; at end of Row 7, finish off: 10 sc.

Edging: With **right** side facing, working in end of rows, and using standard hook; join Variegated with sc in first row; sc in next 5 rows, 2 sc in last row; sc in each sc across Row 7; working in end of rows, 2 sc in same row, sc in next 6 rows; ch 1, turn Hat with Body down, working in free loops of sts on Rnd 3 of Band *(Fig. 2a, page 34)*, slip st in each st around; join with slip st to first ch, finish off.

Fold Brim up.

General Instructions

ABBREVIATIONS

BP	Back Post
BPdc	Back Post double crochet(s)
BPsc	Back Post single crochet(s)
ch(s)	chain(s)
cm	centimeters
dc	double crochet(s)
FP	Front Post
FPdc	Front Post double crochet(s)
FPtr	Front Post treble crochet(s)
Fsc	Foundation single crochet(s)
hdc	half double crochet(s)
mm	millimeters
Rnd(s)	Round(s)
sc	single crochet(s)
sp(s)	space(s)
st(s)	stitch(es)
YO	yarn over

★ — work instructions following ★ as many **more** times as indicated in addition to the first time.

† to † — work all instructions from first † to second † **as many** times as specified.

( ) or [ ] — work enclosed instructions **as many** times as specified by the number immediately following **or** work all enclosed instructions in the stitch or space indicated **or** contains explanatory remarks.

colon (:) — the number(s) given after a colon at the end of a row or round denote(s) the number of stitches or spaces you should have on that row or round.

CROCHET HOOKS												
U.S.	B-1	C-2	D-3	E-4	F-5	G-6	H-8	I-9	J-10	K-10½	N	P	Q
Metric - mm	2.25	2.75	3.25	3.5	3.75	4	5	5.5	6	6.5	9	10	15

▮▯▯▯ **BEGINNER**	Projects for first-time crocheters using basic stitches. Minimal shaping.
▮▮▯▯ **EASY**	Projects using yarn with basic stitches, repetitive stitch patterns, simple color changes, and simple shaping and finishing.
▮▮▮▯ **INTERMEDIATE**	Projects using a variety of techniques, such as basic lace patterns or color patterns, mid-level shaping and finishing.
▮▮▮▮ **EXPERIENCED**	Projects with intricate stitch patterns, techniques and dimension, such as non-repeating patterns, multi-color techniques, fine threads, small hooks, detailed shaping and refined finishing.

GAUGE

Exact gauge is **essential** for proper size. Before beginning your project, make the sample swatch given in the individual instructions in the yarn and hook specified. After completing the swatch, measure it, counting your stitches and rows/rounds carefully. If your swatch is larger or smaller than specified, **make another, changing hook size to get the correct gauge**. Keep trying until you find the size hook that will give you the specified gauge.

MARKERS

Markers are used to help distinguish the beginning of each round being worked. Place a 2" (5 cm) scrap piece of yarn before the first stitch of each round, moving yarn or marker after each round is worked Markers are also placed in a stitch to mark placement of increases.

JOINING WITH SC

When instructed to join with sc, begin with a slip knot on hook. Insert hook in stitch or space indicated, YO and pull up a loop, YO and draw through both loops on hook.

CROCHET TERMINOLOGY	
UNITED STATES	INTERNATIONAL
slip stitch (slip st) =	single crochet (sc)
single crochet (sc) =	double crochet (dc)
half double crochet (hdc) =	half treble crochet (htr)
double crochet (dc) =	treble crochet (tr)
treble crochet (tr) =	double treble crochet (dtr)
double treble crochet (dtr) =	triple treble crochet (ttr)
triple treble crochet (tr tr) =	quadruple treble crochet (qtr)
skip =	miss

Yarn Weight Symbol & Names	LACE 0	SUPER FINE 1	FINE 2	LIGHT 3	MEDIUM 4	BULKY 5	SUPER BULKY 6
Type of Yarns in Category	Fingering, 10-count crochet thread	Sock, Fingering Baby	Sport, Baby	DK, Light Worsted	Worsted, Afghan, Aran	Chunky, Craft, Rug	Bulky, Roving
Crochet Gauge* Ranges in Single Crochet to 4" (10 cm)	32-42 double crochets**	21-32 sts	16-20 sts	12-17 sts	11-14 sts	8-11 sts	5-9 sts
Advised Hook Size Range	Steel*** 6,7,8 Regular hook B-1	B-1 to E-4	E-4 to 7	7 to I-9	I-9 to K-10.5	K-10.5 to M-13	M-13 and larger

*GUIDELINES ONLY: The chart above reflects the most commonly used gauges and hook sizes for specific yarn categories.

** Lace weight yarns are usually crocheted on larger-size hooks to create lacy openwork patterns. Accordingly, a gauge range is difficult to determine. Always follow the gauge stated in your pattern.

*** Steel crochet hooks are sized differently from regular hooks—the higher the number the smaller the hook, which is the reverse of regular hook sizing.

BACK RIDGE

Work only in loops indicated by arrows *(Fig. 1)*.

Fig. 1

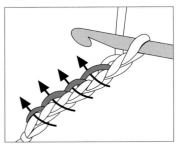

FREE LOOPS

After working in back or front loops only on a round, there will be a ridge of unused loops, called free loops. Later, when instructed to work in free loops of the same round, work in these loops *(Fig. 2a)*. When instructed to work in free loops of a chain, work in loops indicated by arrow *(Fig. 2b)*.

Fig. 2a

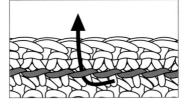

Fig. 2b

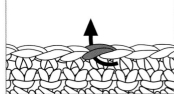

BACK OR FRONT LOOP ONLY

Work only in loop(s) indicated by arrow *(Fig. 3)*.

Fig. 3

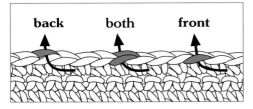

WORKING IN SPACE BEFORE A STITCH

When instructed to work in space before a stitch or in spaces between stitches, insert hook in space indicated by arrow *(Fig. 4)*.

Fig. 4

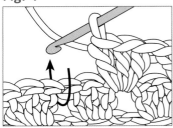

POST STITCH

Work around the post of the stitch indicated, inserting the hook in the direction of the arrow *(Fig. 5)*.

Fig. 5

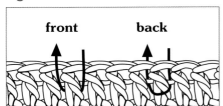

WORKING IN FRONT OF A STITCH

Work in stitch or space indicated, inserting hook in direction of arrow *(Fig. 6)*.

Fig. 6

REVERSE SINGLE CROCHET

(abbreviated reverse sc)

Working from **left** to **right**, ★ insert hook in st to **right** of hook *(Fig. 7a)*, YO and draw through, under and to the left of loop on hook (2 loops on hook) *(Fig. 7b)*, YO and draw through both loops on hook *(Fig. 7c)* (**reverse sc made**, *Fig. 7d)*; repeat from ★ around.

Fig. 7a

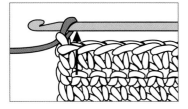

Fig. 7b

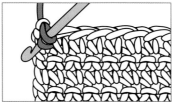

Fig. 7c

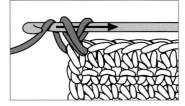

Fig. 7d

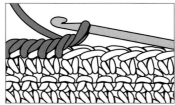

POM-POM

Cut a piece of cardboard 3" (7.5 cm) square. Wind yarn around the cardboard approximately 70-80 times *(Fig. 8a)*. Carefully slip the yarn off the cardboard and firmly tie an 18" (45.5 cm) length of yarn around the middle *(Fig. 8b)*. Leave the yarn ends long enough to attach the Pom-Pom. Cut the loops on both ends and trim the Pom-Pom into a smooth ball *(Fig. 8c)*.

Fig. 8a

Fig. 8b

Fig. 8c

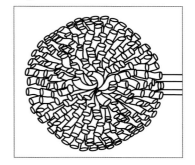

WHIPSTITCH

With **wrong** sides together, sew through both pieces once to secure the beginning of the seam, leaving an ample yarn end to weave in later. Insert the needle from **front** to **back** through the inside loops on each piece *(Fig. 9)*. Bring the needle around and insert it from **front** to **back** through the next strands on both pieces. Repeat along the edge, being careful to match stitches and rounds.

Fig. 9

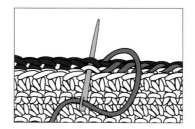

YARN INFORMATION

Each project in this leaflet was made using medium weight yarn. Any brand of medium weight yarn may be used. It is best to refer to the yardage/meters when determining how many skeins to purchase. Remember, to arrive at the finished size, it is the GAUGE/TENSION that is important, not the brand of yarn.

For your convenience, listed below are the specific yarns used to create our photography models.

PURPLE TEXTURES
Lion Brand® Vanna's Choice®
Variegated - #303 Purple Mist
Purple - #147 Purple

ORANGE FLOWER
Caron® Simply Soft®
Peach - #9737 Light Country Peach
Caron® Simply Soft® Brites
Orange - #9605 Mango

TAN PLAID
Bernat® Satin
Tan - #04010 Camel
Brown - #04011 Sable

YELLOW PUFFS
Caron® Simply Soft®
Yellow - #9726 Soft Yellow
Caron® Simply Soft® Brites
Gold - #9606 Lemonade

RIPPLES AND RUFFLES
Premier™ Yarns Deborah Norville Collection
Everyday Soft Worsted Prints
Variegated - #ED 100-01 Nursery
Premier™ Yarns Deborah Norville Collection
Everyday Soft Worsted Solids
Green - #ED 100-04 Baby Green

BLUE TUNISIAN
Red Heart® Soft Baby Steps™
Variegated - #9935 Blue Earth Print
Blue - #9800 Baby Blue

We have made every effort to ensure that these instructions are accurate and complete. We cannot, however, be responsible for human error, typographical mistakes, or variations in individual work.

Production Team: Instructional/Technical Editors - Linda Daley, Sarah J. Green, Cathy Hardy, Lois J. Long, and Lindsay Diane White; Editorial Writer - Susan McManus Johnson; Graphic Artist - Katherine Laughlin; Photo Stylist - Sondra Daniel; and Photographer - Ken West.